FAMILIES

My Mum

Katie Dicker

D1425837

Explore the world with **Popcorn** - your complete first non-fiction library.

Look out for more titles in the Popcorn range. All books have the same format of simple text and striking images. Text is carefully matched to the pictures to help readers to identify and understand key vocabulary.
www.waylandbooks.co.uk/popcorn

Published in 2015 by Wayland
Copyright © Wayland 2015

Wayland
Hachette Children's Books
338 Euston Road
London NW1 3BH

Wayland Australia
Level 17/207 Kent Street
Sydney NSW 2000

Produced for Wayland by
White-Thomson Publishing Ltd
www.wtpub.co.uk
+44 (0)843 208 7460

Editor: Katie Dicker
Designer: Amy Sparks
Picture researcher: Katie Dicker
Series consultant: Kate Ruttle
Design concept: Paul Cherrill

British Library Cataloguing in Publication Data
Dicker, Katie.
   My mum. -- (Popcorn)
   1. Mothers--Juvenile literature.
   2. Mother and child--Juvenile literature.
   I. Title II. Series
   306.8'743-dc22

First published in 2010 by Wayland

ISBN: 978 0 7502 8882 8

Wayland is a division of Hachette Children's Books,
an Hachette UK company.
www.hachette.co.uk

Printed and bound in China

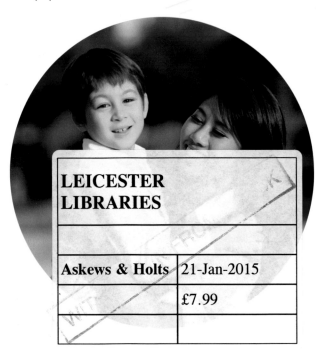

Picture Credits: **Corbis:** Eric Audras/PhotoAlto 9, Andersen Ross/Blend Images 13, Tom Grill 14, Moodboard 17; **Dreamstime:** Monkey Business Images cover/5/21, Konstantin Sutyagin 2/6/22r, Kameel4u 18/22m; **Getty Images:** Clandestini 7, Stephen Wilkes 8, Andrew Olney 10, Blend Images/ Annika Erickson 11, Image Source 15; **Photolibrary:** Edis Jurcys 16, Paul Paul 19, Willy de l'Horme/ Photononstop 20; **Shutterstock:** Monkey Business Images 1/12, Jaimie Duplass 4/22l.

Every effort has been made to clear copyright. Should there be any inadvertent omission, please apply to the publisher for rectification.

Contents

What is a mum?

Your mum is the person who made you with your dad. She is sometimes called your birth mum.

You grew inside your birth mum's tummy before you were born.

Kuda's mum is expecting another baby in a few months.

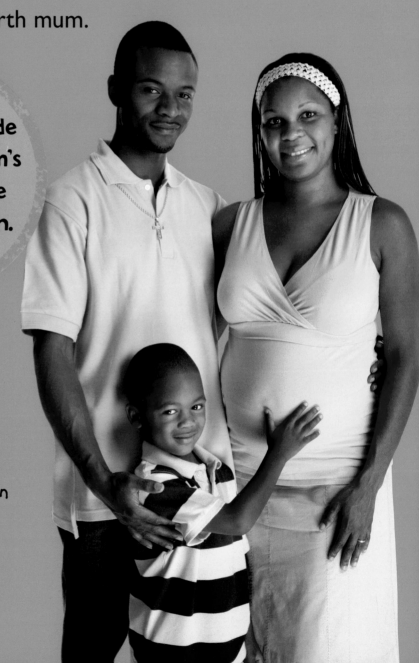

A mum can also be someone
who isn't your birth mum.
This mum may live with your
dad and help to care for you.

Billy lives with his mum, his dad and his sister, Sophia.

Different mums

You have a stepmum if your birth dad marries someone who isn't your birth mum.

Oscar's stepmum has looked after him since he was a baby.

Some children don't know their birth mum because she has died or because she has moved away.

Clare is adopted. She doesn't live
with her birth parents, but she calls
her new parents Mum and Dad.

Clare's new mum and dad are going to look after her.

Someone new

If you have a stepmum, or your mum has a new partner, it can be difficult to get used to the changes in your family.

Toby didn't like his stepmum at first. It took time to get to know each other, but now they get on well.

Talk to your parents about how
you feel. They will understand
that the changes might be hard
for you to deal with.

**Your mum may
have found a new
partner because
it makes her
feel happy.**

George felt jealous because he was
used to having his mum to himself.

 Single mums

Amelia's dad doesn't live with them any more. Amelia helps her mum to look after her brothers and sisters instead.

Amelia tries to help her mum with jobs at home, too.

Single mums have to go to
work to buy all the things
their family needs.

Omar can't wait for his mum to get home from work.

Help and advice

Your mum has learnt a lot of things in her life. She's a good person to ask if you need help with something.

What would you find difficult to do without your mum's help?

Your mum will care for you as you grow up. She will also help to teach you how to do things for yourself.

When Hannah cut her knee, her mum helped to make it better.

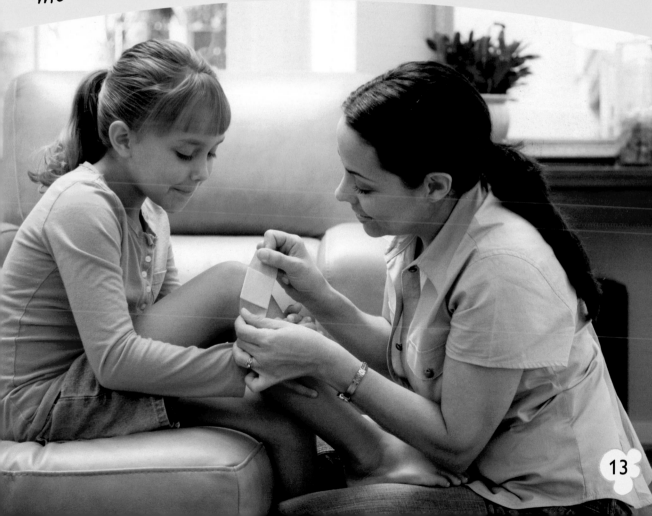

Time to talk

Your mum may be very busy, but she still loves you. She will make time for you if you need her.

Talk to your mum if you are worried about something.

Amy's mum gives her time to talk about how she's feeling.

Rosie's mum has taught Rosie to tell the truth. If she breaks something, Rosie lets her mum know.

Rosie's mum was upset that the glass was broken, but she thanked Rosie for being honest.

Working together

Mums work very hard to care for their family. You can make their lives easier by offering to help.

Charlie tries to help at home because his mum is busy with a new baby.

16

Helping in the house can be fun. If everyone helps, there is more time to spend together at the end of the day.

Kia helps her mum to clean the kitchen floors.

Understanding rules

It can sometimes be hard to get along with your mum. You may find it difficult to accept your mum's rules.

Parents have rules because they want to keep you safe and healthy.

Why do you think Poppy's mum sends her to bed before her older brothers and sisters?

Most rules are there to
keep you safe. If you don't
understand a rule, talk to
your mum about it.

Gemma's mum let her walk to school, but she had to
go with her big brother, and use the zebra crossing.

A special person

Learning how to get along with people is an important skill. If you and your mum get on well, it can bring you both a lot of happiness.

Your mum thinks of you even when you are apart.

Your mum is part of your family. You care for her, and she cares for you. This makes her very special.

How do you like to spend time with your mum?

Thinking about mums

1. Look at these photographs showing some of the children and their mums featured in this book. Can you answer these questions? Look back through the book if you need a reminder.

1. What does Kuda's mum have inside her tummy?

2. How long has Oscar known his stepmum?

3. Does Poppy go to bed at the same time as her brothers and sisters?

Answers: 1. Kuda's mum has a baby in her tummy.
2. Oscar has known his stepmum since he was a baby.
3. No, Poppy goes to bed before her older brothers and sisters.

2. What do you think is the best thing about having a mum? Make a list of your ideas.

Someone to comfort me when I'm sad

Looks after me

Knows the things I like to eat

3. Imagine that you've gone on a holiday without your mum. Write a letter or postcard to your mum saying all the things you miss about her. What are you looking forward to doing with your mum when you get home?

Dear Mum,

We've been to the zoo today.
I wish you were here so you could see all the amazing animals.

I fell over and cut my knee.
It really hurt. Grandad doesn't have special plasters like yours.

I'm having a good time, but I miss your cooking. Can't wait to have your fish pie again.

Love Tim

Mum
15 Wentworth Road
Dulchester
TB6 8AZ

Glossary

adopted when someone lives with parents who are not their birth parents

birth dad the man who made you with your birth mum

birth mum the woman who made you with your birth dad

deal to be able to handle a difficult situation

honest to tell the truth

marries when someone becomes a husband or a wife to someone else

parents your mum and dad

partner the person that an adult loves and chooses to live with

single mum a mum who raises her children on her own, without the help of a partner

stepmum someone who marries your birth dad (but is not your birth mum)

Index